A
DARK AGE

A DARK AGE

WES MAGEE

Rosalind,
Good to say Hello....
in Winchester!

[signature: Wes Magee]

BLACKSTAFF PRESS

[1988]

By the same author:

Poems

Poetry Introduction 2
Urban Gorilla
No Man's Land (Poetry Book Society Recommendation)

For children

Oliver, the daring birdman (story)
The real spirit of Christmas (play)
The space beasts (poems)

British Library Cataloguing in Publication Data

Magee, Wes
    A dark age.
    I. Title
    821'.914   PR6063.A328
    ISBN 0–85640–256–7

Published by Blackstaff Press Limited,
3 Galway Park, Dundonald, BT16 0AN
with the assistance of
the Arts Council of Northern Ireland

Contents

'He peered forward past the sail to see
what lay at the other end of the lake, but it
was so long, and there was such a flashing
from the water that he could not see if the
line of darkness had an ending.'

(*The Inheritors*, William Golding)

A New Year

Night comes jackbooting through the wood
And the sky roars at trees and a dying light.
Pregnant, the river is gulped into darkness
While sheep, like town lights, blot out one by one.

In the house, beneath blanketing thatch,
Twenty of us gather to see the New Year in.
We talk; wine runs away with itself;
Wailing demons are trapped up the chimney.

Midnight first-foots with a bombardment of snow.
The wind is celebrating madly.
Owls rattle in barns as we clasp hands
And another year is born in a blitz of stars.

(Totleigh Barton, Devon)

Sheep, buried

(for George MacBeth, who dug)

Overnight, an airborne invasion.
Blizzard's shock troops have taken the low hills
    And this morning's monochrome standard
Unfurls stiffly across a raw landscape.
    Colour has been confined to barracks.
A steel wind keens the no man's land between
Snowfield and sky: a shivering of distance.

    Rag-clad, like Siberian lifers,
We stump uphill to where the field's hedge
    Has vanished beneath a crested drift.
Here lie sheep, buried. Instinct led them to
    Expect shelter from the savage storm.
Like punters we must thrust six-foot canes down
Through snow to prod the earth's frozen muscle.

    We string out, figures on a bleak ridge.
Shove, bend, haul and straighten. Repeat. Repeat.
    The ewe's body, when struck, feels tough
As a tractor tyre. Our shouts echo long
    Before shovels arrive and we dig,
Fox-holing in a winter's warfare, and
There she is, wool ice-starred, her nose snow-slushed.

    We manhandle her clear, our curses
Kindling the air. A kick and she staggers
    Towards a scaup of field where snow lies thin.
Now we lean on shovels, the silence sharp,
    A panorama brittle with frost.
The sun emerges, pallid survivor,
A prisoner led out for exercise.

2

Winter domestic

Drowned winter; the lounge curtains tugged tight
Against her ragamuffin migrants
– Hail, sledge-heavy sleet, hooligan gales.
Clamorous they importune the house.
Held in the standard lamp's tent of light
I huddle before a roaring fire.

A Venusian beamed down to this room
Would note 'papers cat-curled at my feet,
The children hibernating in rugs.
His report would describe how the being
Brandished a blackened rod to control
A many-tongued, log-devouring beast.

Leaving, he would have seen dark weather
Massed high above a thrashed Atlantic
And heard the wind's collection of cries;
Observed, also, landscapes mugged with snow.
Later I kill the lamp, watch fire-light
Reel off walls like a Christmas Eve drunk.

Visitant, cruising the hushed spaceways,
Return and view this room's gloomed mirror,
The way my image pools with shadow,
How glisks of light originate a skull.
Let us talk of galactic blackness
And stars flung like glitter to the void.

Visiting Belfast

1947

The Lisburn Road. As a boy
I served in the 'General Stores'
Scooping sugar from a sack
That stood unyielding
And solid as a bomb.

The cheese-cutter's handles
Were shaped for gripping.
Arms quivered as I pulled hard down
On the wire until cheese lay
Sliced on the white slab.

With knife held low I would
Sneak behind the counter
And stab my uncle in the back.
The blade recoiled on its spring.
King Billy ruled gable ends.

1977

Early morning at the docks
And there are soldiers
Who clearly mean business
But no taxis or buses
As a strike stuns the city.

Outside the dock gates
Men stand in doleful groups.
A soft mizzle drifts off the lough
Where gulls wheel, waiting.
The wharfs lie idle.

From his sand-bagged roof
An observer scans the streets.
Derelict houses are shuttered
With corrugated iron.
Skag, and Billy, rule all the walls.

The Irish jokes

They spread alarmingly, ethnic caricatures
Featuring Irishmen as thick Micks with huge hands.
They are the club comic's cheap laugh, swelling his sad
Repertoire of in-law, wife, Jew, and blue funnies.
Daily they creep up and jab your shoulder, as now:
How can you spot an Irishman in the car wash?
    He's the one on the bicycle!
Germ-like they pass from mouth to mouth, a verbal 'flu
Which children quickly catch and bring home loud from school.

Perhaps it's the notion of being green as a Treen
Or living on a leaky raft in the Atlantic
Or sheer despair at the chain-reaction killings:
Humour as rank as marsh-gas when all solutions
Founder against nailed sheets of corrugated iron.
One can but listen and smile as the jokes hit home,
    Bullets of fun leaving you weak
At the knee-caps. They will continue to trouble,
Like laughter heard in bars where bombs burst just last year.

Cattle trucks

1

Rural Ulster in World War Two
and deep in a green-hilled landscape
I whittled away a sun-buttered summer
far from the sand-bagged shelters of Dundee
and doodlebugs thundering above the docks.

Once, my father took my hand
and together we helped drive cattle
down Duck Street
towards the one-platformed railway station,
even then a museum piece.

In my fist a stripped switch
with which I whisked one bullock
that stopped to peer
into the tiniest post office in County Armagh.
Another generously mucked the gutter.

How those beasts lingered, dawdled.
And slapping their hammock-slung stomachs
I heard depth-charges
crumping fathoms deep in the U-boat ocean.

2

   Beside the rusted track
farmers gathered for good crack
while their men diverted cattle
ruminal for the legendary grass.
The platform was rapidly
splattered with glaur.

   Up ramps
the animals were herded;
skittish, and baulking
at the closed trucks' gloom
until persuaded with blackthorns.
Each truck was filled as positively
as a corned beef tin.

   I remember
the strawed floors,
sodden and soured,
and how knives of light
sliced through cracks in wall-boards.
Then each truck was chained shut.

   The engine steamed
while the guard confused
his red and green flags
until with a violent jerk
couplings yanked rigid
and the engine's chimney
erupted creamy clots of smoke.

   Slowly
the trucks squealed past
and on up the track.
The frantic mooing died away
where trees converged.

3

During that summer, I now know,
similar cattle trucks lined up
beside platforms throughout Europe.

Instead of cattle; people.
Rifle butts replaced the whacking blackthorns
and there must have been, too,

that same retch as the engine thrust forward,
and then the certainty of the incarcerated
that what lay ahead was unimaginable.

Up-line you would have heard their cries
as they stood in dense darkness, cowed,
the floorboards drowning in human waste.

4

This summer's day, as I write,
   the century steams towards
its unknown destination.
   In the garden my boy
is chasing butterflies,
   his hands clap-clapping
at their dusty fragility.

No more *that* sort of joy;
   just thoughts of cattle trucks
and where they now rest,
   unmaintained, forgotten
in lost sidings
   where weeds grow thigh-high
and the sun stares, unblinking.

The trucks' doors are warped,
   hinges broken,
wisps of straw cradling memories
   of hooves, and feet.
The splintered sides
   are scrawled with chalk,
named destinations of the past –

Majdanek, Treblinka, Auschwitz;
the slaughter-houses of Belfast.

A field in West Germany

National Servicemen on a bender
We drove south from our barracks in Soltau;
A day's leave, and freedom from boots, khaki.
Every *gasthaus* was a filling station
Where we tanked-up on Hensen beer and stuffed
Away hunks of dark bread and black sausage.
In one bar a drunk pulled a revolver
And we left at the double, chairs crashing.
On the road our sole concern was roaring
The army version of 'Lilli Marlene'.

As daylight drained we followed a sign for
'Belsen'. Bubbly drunk we came loud to it,
Our pockets bulging with bottles, and stood
In a field in West Germany staring
At the high mounds and acres of lush grass.
Beyond massed pines the sky was a red wash.
Each fell silent, caging his own unease
As the day died. A deep gloom grew until
We were aware at last of the wind's keen
And how in that place no bird sang or flew.

Snapshots at the slate mine
(Aberllefenni, North Wales)

1. Signs of dereliction

Sheep droppings in
    the 'General Office'.

A fractured water pipe
    gushing refreshment.

Wasps' nest in the back seat
    of a mangled car.

Rusty bogie wheels
    fused with the iron earth.

In an outbuilding
    a piano dumb with damp.

2. The slate garden

gripping
the slate
spangles of ochre lichen

between
the slate
grass as dry as twine

above
the slate
tiny ferns, bled white

covering
the slate
mini eider-downs of moss

beneath
the slate
bright orange fungus

beyond
the slate
armies of nettles

massing

3. Ruined dwelling

The skeleton of a roof remains;
laths, and rags of sodden plaster.

Sheep sleep where grass has laid
wall-to-wall carpeting.

Above the wrecked fire-place
a flag of floral wallpaper.

4. Tunnel

The hill's side is pierced;
a black O into which
rusting rails vanish.

Fridge-chilled air sharpens
a percussion of water drops;
the walls are skull splitters.

From Guinness blackness you hear
a distant crump and rumble;
the hill's slate heart collapsing.

5. How to scree ski

At the top
take a deep breath
then leap far out.
Landing
dig heels deep in
and lean backwards.
At once
take giant strides
downhill.
Your feet
sink into slate,
ankles vanish.
Extended arms,
like wings,
give you balance.
At the bottom
white plimsolls
have turned grey.
Landslides
flood your tracks.
The scree slope
gnashes its tiny teeth
and a billion fragments

resettle.

6. Miranda, age 6, on a still day

The lake is a sheet of tin.
'Do Not Disturb' has been strung
across the sleeping hills.
Kestrels are pinned
against an impassive sky.

Far below, on the slate,
you have fallen, grazed your knee.
Thin cries reach me.
Distance. All I can do
is snap the scene, hold you, fixed.

From a barn

Atomic sunlight burns its way
Into the barn's mud-thickened walls.
A cat sleeks across the door-gap.
And now catch the eye-wrenching flick
Of screaming swifts before they thrust
Beyond the roof's alarming sag.
In sunbeams dust slowly revolves,
Universe within universe
Of motes intent on their turning,
Knowing only silence and crude
Inexhaustible energy.

If a clock ticked loud here you would
Know this moment being nailed into
Time's long coffin, and comprehend
The pitiless drift of matter
To that moment when suns explode
And create a furious dark.
Even then dust will revolve, prove
Indestructible as it turns
With relentless indifference.
And now storm heat builds in the barn:
Scent of ash falls out from the air.

Old stick
(*in memory of my father*)

It stands in the hall, the blackthorn stick
    You brought from Ulster years ago
When coming to convert the English.
Each Sunday you preached with pentecostal fire
    Fisting the pulpit until it shook.
        Satan took some stick.

You were the fundamentalist who
    Sporting shamrock could be stage Mick
Or, with hair greased and soot dabbed below
Your nose, Hitler raving hilariously.
    An argument with a car robbed you
        Of that ebullience.

Old photographs now remind me of
    The non-conforming reverend
Who could pose with lampshade for a hat
Or tote a broom rifle as 'Ulster's last hope':
    Those, and that uncompromising stick
        Standing in the hall.

'A chaos to tame'
(in memory of Maurice Carpenter)

It was how you named your house,
A place cram-full with papers
And the untamable dog
You saved from being put down.
The local rag featured *that*
But not, I think, your poems.

Our lives were wholly diverse:
You the relapsed communist
Who married three times and took
To writing plays for a group
Of feckless local youngsters.
Thirty years stood between us.

When I called at your study
You sputtered about Auden,
Parton Street and the Thirties.
I never did find the chair.
Once you dragged the dog to a
Television interview;

Unstoppable it howled, barked,
And laid waste the studio.
At our reading in Devon
Your head whacked against a beam;
White hair stained pink. Resolute
You read on and drank till dawn.

I recall 'doing' Paisley's
Voice on the phone demanding
Support for the Orange cause.
You bawled back, stentorian.
I cherish your angry note
Addressed to 'an Ulster git'.

20

Hold dear, too, those thin booklets
Of poems and plays; scant reward
From a lifetime of wrangles
With unhelpful publishers.
I was writing when told you
Had died. The day grew chaotic,

The wild world remained untamed.

Legend
(for Jack O' Legs)

He was a freak, so tall he could gawk
Through upstairs bedroom windows and talk
With villagers as they lay in bed.

Helpful, too. One snow-marooned winter
He strode buried fields, stole sacks of flour
From a distant mill and fed his friends.

That act was decisive; the miller
Gathered toughs, ambushed him in a copse.
He was bound, knifed, and his eyes gouged out.

Before the end they granted one wish,
Handed him a bow from which he loosed
A shaft. Where it fell – three miles away –

They agreed to dig his grave. And so
To the main business of that cold day.
Six men strove to hang him from an oak.

The shock treatment

It was a Sunday afternoon ritual,
Tea with the 'man across the road'; Stalin's house.
There is no forgetting his heavy features
Or reddish moustache bristled like a yard brush.
Tea in the parlour meant brown sauce sandwiches
And cocoa the colour of mahogany.

Avuncular, we would produce a teak box
As if displaying a saint's casked remains to
Goggling peasants. Years ago, yet I recall
Its immaculate mortise and tenon joints,
Iron winder, and a lead snaking from each end.
The leads terminated in brass tubes. 'Grip them.'

My hands closed on cold metal. The winder turned
And I felt current flow through fingers, wrists,
On up my arms until the sinews tingled.
Faster he wound; rubberised bones knotted tight.
Neither shakings nor pleading would release my grip.
When he stopped I was on my knees, limbs unhinged.

Lodestone, that box magnetised me each Sunday,
Its magic shock a pain to be savoured.
The winter before we left that town I saw
Tasselled curtains drawn at his windows and a
Black coffin borne to an immaculate hearse.
There is no forgetting that, or the snow's chill.

A child's white magic in the gym

I will cartwheel
Past changelings in the nut-brown wood.

I will belly-crawl
When witches fly for the yellow-face moon.

I will forward roll
To escape the werewolf's blood-red fangs.

I will back-flip
As ghosts gather in the dead-grey garden.

I will vault the horse
If bogeymen tap at the white-washed windows.

I will handstand
And confuse the warlocks on the grass-green hill.

I will freeze
When the teacher's silver whistle sounds.

The wolf child

Father told me it is a girl
Yet 'Feral' has been poker-worked
Into the wood above her cage
And that's not a girl's name, I know.
    Was she *really* found in a wolf's den?

I must have been here for an hour
And seen nothing but her scratched back
As she squats in that far corner.
How hard and small the shaved head seems.
    Is it true her eyes glow in the dark?

Soon mother will come to fetch me.
India is terribly hot
And I'm thirsty as the devil.
Even her water-bowl is fouled.
    Why doesn't she howl as they report?

The stink reminds me of the byre
Back on Uncle's farm in Devon
Her spine looks like the Pennine Chain
In my Geography book. Ho Hum.
    When *is* she going to eat that raw meat?

Romulus and Remus sounded
Exciting but this is plain dull.
They say she bites, but I refuse
To believe she runs on all fours.
    What *can* be delaying my mother?

I'll rattle the bars with this stick.
You see, not even a whimper.
How can one tell if she's breathing?
Why doesn't she turn and face me?
    Can't she sense that I am here, waiting?

An island story

Clifftop grass is silken; sheets of shantung:
The sea's rucked quilt envelops a vast bed.
Sky's scrubbed and shining face beams. Our fingers
Are stained silver; stem juice of plucked flowers.

Such summer's day that revives my childhood
When story-book islands spelled adventure
– ducats buried in sand dunes, dank caverns,
Lamps blinking at night from castle turrets.

Feeling sunshine and sea-breeze gild our skin
We loll in luxury. This hour is worth
A month of Sundays . . . the surf a mumble,
Gulls peeling off the cliffs . . . their plangent cries.

We lob stones and watch as waves gulp, swallow,
Then close lambent lips. A skylark outlines
Its upward flight-path . . . erratic as my
Daughter's drawing in her dot-to-dot book.

Our afternoon idles towards evening.
Sky's face swells ogreish with purple blotches;
Blundering winds topple castles of cloud.
A deep, long-buried sense of foreboding

Surfaces as lights star the horizon.
Distances close. Darkness washes up drifts
Of fright, thrill, mystery. Gelid moonlight
Casts memory's gold coins in my outstretched palm.

Mermaid

She was dragged from the sea,
   Dropped boneless on damp sand,
Hair a weedy tatter.
   Bathers stared as a man
Worked her over until
   She retched. The sea left her.
Then, flopped on a stretcher,
   She was carted away,
A red blanket trailing.

We resumed beach cricket
   While others dared again
The waves on floats, air-beds.
   Beyond the rusting pier
An anchored warship lay.
   I never learned if she
Lived or died, but at school
   Featured her in my
'Summer Holiday' report.

The incident survives
   While all else that year has
Been swept sea-clean by a
   Tide of forgetfulness.
I recall shoving through
   The crush, how her slack mouth
Spewed into the bronze beach,
   And the way she fish-gasped,
Drowning in strange stuff, air.

On the esplanade

Senses withered all year in town
   Cannot assimilate this effervescence
– the sea-breeze soaked with ozone,
Clouds so fresh they hurt your eyes
And are confused with foaming rollers.
   Whack of flags beats the ear,
As do those whip-crack ropes
Against the masts and cleats of yachts.

   Everything eats. Gulls devour a groyne.
      Man gobbles a girl who, glowingly,
         Wears nothing but an orange life-jacket.
   Ices cream the brine-dried lips of children.

Unable to contain the day's zip and fizz
   I search for relief,
Head for the Gents' cool, moist cavern.
To enter I step over a picnic spread
– egg sandwiches piled high like Pisan towers.
   An extended family, hard up against their car,
Follow my legs with crazed eyes.
Mouths bulge with grub. Oh, the taste! The taste!

The football replays

*'Football in England is a grey game
played on grey days for grey people.'*
                    (Rodney Marsh)

1. Ball girl

A pre-match bonus
she runs onto the pitch
wearing white shorts, red shirt,
and toe-punts a ball
towards the centre circle.

Stuff *that!* the thousands mutter
and then realise
that beneath her shirt
she is wearing not a thing.
Breasts bouncing loose!

Sudden in-whistle of breath
and every eye hard-on
that patch of red cloth:
a silence you could ignite
before she canters off,

legs hacking sideways,
to a growing, primitive roar.
Minutes later World War Three kicks off
and we're left with that vision;
soft flesh, unfettered, free.

                    (*County Ground, Swindon*)

2. A day out

Years since I was last at Wembley
and now I'm back
with forty urban estate youngsters
who have chanted, cheered
and vomited their way up the M4.

The match is unwatchable:
the sheer restlessness
of treble-voiced fuss-pots
sends two of us in search of a bar
below the decks of this concrete liner.

Once there we must pull rank
to push through the gangs
of thirteen-year-olds
boozing on bottled brown ale.
A pleasant place, I think you said.

When it's all over
there's the missing boy to find,
the duffle bags left among litter
and one tiny tearaway
who has lost his trousers.

It was the longest day
which even at this remove of years
can conjure up a headache.
I recall our loud return;
the lights of Swindon never so desired.

(Schoolboy International; Wembley)

3. Hwyl

The final whistle imminent
  with the Swans two up
    and arrogant.
      In stands and on terraces
      fifteen thousand fans
      are one-voiced,
        a Welsh choir
          whose anthem
            rises
              full-throated
            to the night.
            The match flows on,
          a mere back-drop
        to this event
        of greater passion.
      A Celtic fervour
     proclaims itself
   and the moon
inclines an ear to listen.

                  (Vetch Field, Swansea)

4. A death

Day long the sky wept.
'Who's died?' someone at work asked.

Tonight the porridgy pitch
glistens beneath the floodlights
and players delight in sliding tackles.
One skids stunningly on his bum.

On the terraces a man crumples,
is propped against overcoats
until they shift and he collapses,
face grey as the concrete it greets.
Dentures are out, mouth is dribbling.

Whistles summon the stretcher men
who squelch the touch-line as they run.

The sky is weeping.

(County Ground, Swindon)

32

5. The big drop

He has clambered
   high among
the rusted girders
   of the 'shed'
and from there views
   a Subbuteo-sized
relegation decider.
   The match is tidal
– red waves roll in,
   are repulsed,
roll in again –
   until on the hour
there is a home goal
   to celebrate.
Druid-like his hands
   praise the night.
Falling, he drops
   to what?
Arms? Concrete?
   The game surges:
the fans bay at
   one hundred full moons
which glare from the
   darkness.

(County Ground, Swindon)

An A-Z of couplings

Antonia balled Clive
Deirdre engulfed Fergus
Godfrey humped Ingrid
Jasper kissed Leonora
Marianne nibbled Oswald
Peregrine queened Rodney
Seamus tumbled Ursula
Valerie wanted Xavier

Yrogenous Zones!

An A-Z of headlines

Atomic Blast Cripples Doncaster
Excitable Foreman Garrottes Hooligans
Injured Judge's Kidney Lost
Mad Nun Ousts Pope
Queen Rewrites Shakespeare's Tragedies
Ubiquitous Venusian Worships Xylophone
            Yak Zooms

Macbeth in a provincial town

As Birnam Wood removes to Dunsinane
(Scaffolding and painted planks) there are more
People on stage than in the audience.
For a score of local thespians this
Is *living* in a town light years from London.

It was damp October when we gathered
At a glossed gymnasium to read, and cut,
The play – comprehensive school teachers, wives,
A curate with shoulder-length hair, some gays.
The vaulting horse stood buried beneath coats.

Winter long we worried the words until,
In March the town's Arts Centre became ours.
Frank's set was bland as a Sainsbury's food hall
And the slung spots shone floodlit-football bright.
Chewed speeches triumphed at dress rehearsal.

Our producer freaked, and his raised voice ranted,
'Gentlemen, at least let us have a *good*
Fourth-rate production!' One hour in Paul's
Lounge bar ironed out the lines stitching his brow.
Someone had scrawled 'Bard lives' on the loo wall.

And so to Dunsinane . . . with sticks and twigs.
After six performances our play is
Slick as soap, and tonight there's wine backstage.
Then, in May, to Joan's for a barbecue;
Come autumn we start *The Taming of the Shrew*.

The prince's tale

I have driven through heat
To keep this date with Rapunzel.
Beyond the beyond I climb a hill
Where my ankles are fettered in heather.
Left behind, the car sulks in the sun.

From the crag's split lip
I stare into a wooded valley,
Its slopes a cardigan of greens.
Hidden, a secret river motors around
Boulders shaped like skulls.

And *there* is your tower prison
A finger reaching through trees.
I descend as the day dies
And the sky floods with darkness.
The valley floor is sodden with decay.

At the tower I hiss your name,
'Rapunzel!' The nightland swirls
With whooshing owls and sniggering water.
'Rapunzel!' In answer the moon
Uncoils itself from cloud,

Tumbles a braid of blonde light
Down the tower's rough wall.
My grasping hands rasp on stone.
From the sinister river
A waterfall of screams

And there is the witch,
Eyes the hunting green of a cat.
Her tattered skirts drip water
Like blobs of mercury.
Warty hands of witch close over mine.

The moonlight plait twists, twists.
From the immense tower
I hear your frail voice calling.
The night erodes my sight;
This pictured scene set for ever.

Old pop songs

Like shoes they passed from fashion,
Were dated within the year
Yet decades later those sounds
Unerringly recall times
When you walked footloose in fairgrounds.

That oldie twanging from the
Juke-box has your mouth miming
The singer's each strangled phrase;
Drums, jangly guitars revive
Whole choruses of yeah-yeah-yeahs.

Reservoirs of sentiment
They gush with sparkling young love
And singalong summers, yet
The dream girls remained mere names:
Diana, Peggy Sue, Claudette.

Spinning old seventy-eights
(lyrics murdered by jump, hiss)
Evoke days of El's suede shoes,
Nights at Heartbreak Hotel
And everyone singin' the blues.

Wrecks

1. Exhumations

The car buried behind a wall,
A fish-eyed corpse with foliage
Erasing a famous trade-mark.

In the graveyard bodies are parked.
Headstones bow. Weeds and frost threaten
To destroy the forever names.

All ending up . . . in hushed places
Where only scrap-metal gypsies come
Or detectives with bright spades.

2. The roadshark

This is a deepsea raider,
    The hundred miles per hour shark
Jaguaring the night's depths,
    Green light aglow in its head.

It pulses in the darkness,
    A well-oiled sleekness homing
On female perfumes; walnut
    Interior a bedroom.

The leather-gloved hand now grips
    A knobbed gear-stick, a smooth knee,
Seeks out the organ-stop nipples.
    A hard and gobbling hunger.

And when the loud laughter dies
    . . . a sea-rot, punctured lungs, rust.
Leaves dare to touch, to nuzzle
    This terrible perfection.

3. Dormobile memories

Such a time she had that summer
Parked in the shadow of sand dunes
While the sun dissolved in the sea.
Such nights when two naked figures
Wrestled hard in their sleeping bag,
And her tin sides perspired with love.

Now she stands held fast by bindweed,
Skin peeling where the sun-tan fades
And the spray-on make-up flakes, flakes.
She was a lovers' nest on wheels.
Creaking springs are sole reminder
Of nights when her world bucked and sang.

4. How many?

How many
Were flogged along motorways,
Driven to a final gasp
And shuddering of wrenched parts?

How many
Taken in the night while their
Loved ones slept; then tortured on
Rough roads until their spines snapped?

How many
Perished in secret places
Where only grass and groundsel mourn
The broken bones, the bodies?

How many
Road deaths, victims of the camps
Have we plotted on graphs? How
Many names have we forgotten?

Family ghosts

The weather is Mancunian, the sky swollen, sick.
A day made for apparitions, and I find one
Lurking in the shed, whittling a stick.
      Another hovers over an ancient range while
Drops of water roll and sizzle on the hot plates.
A third charms potatoes from friable soil
And his pipe splutters in the day's drizzle.
      Three ghosts whose blood trickles in my veins
Yet my hands have lost their skills with wood and earth.
      Beyond the window the weather glowers.
The sky grows murky as an ocean's bed.
Darkness. Surrounded by typewriters and telephones
I watch my spectres fade. Ghost-grey
The shades of distance spread and spread.

Darkness

Children, we burrowed beneath blankets
And knew the bed's hot darkness before
Sheets entwined our heads, left us gasping.

Worse still was waking after midnight
To glimpse a gaunt man behind the door
Where my dressing-gown usually hung.

Once, a girl and I crawled into the
Tar blackness of an air-raid shelter
Then fled as a feathered-thing squawked, flew.

Now *my* children creep down that same path,
Test darkness, tiptoe the line between
Inquisitiveness and speechless fear.

While touring old coastal defences
They insist on descending steep steps
To explore a dank, brick-strewn tunnel.

I demur, preferring the seascape
With its total sound-surround of gulls
But am dragged to a mildewy gloom

Where voices echo and birds have died.
Again that icy shiver. Silenced
We cling to each other, stumble deep

Into a tomb. Wide eyes conjure up
Unspeakable shapes in the foul air
And a finger of bone, beckoning.

An evening

Crept in unseen, an evening.
On his back lawn a man stands.

The shrubbery holds its breath.
A fuchsia glows in the porch.

Leaves smoulder at garden ends.
Traffic, transistors murmur

Almost below the threshold
Of hearing. The sky deepens.

Lean from an upstairs window
And inhale this serene hour

Before night climbs the earth's curve
And the summer closes down.

Long may such moments endure
Where the years pile and darken.

Acknowledgements

Acknowledgements are due to the editors of the following journals, anthologies and small press publications in which a number of the poems have appeared:
Ambit, Beloit Poetry Journal (USA), *Country Life, Encounter, Helix* (Australia), *Hertfordshire Countryside, The Honest Ulsterman, Irish Press, Iron, Kudos, Michigan Quarterly Review* (USA), *New Edinburgh Review, The New Review, Outposts, Pacific Quarterly* (New Zealand), *Palantir, P.E.N. Broadsheet, Poetry Chicago* (USA), *Poetry Review, Poetry Wales, Priapus Press, Quarto, Samphire, Sceptre Press, The Scotsman, South-West Review, The Tablet, Xenia Press*. 'Cattle trucks' and 'The shock treatment' were broadcast on BBC Radio 3.
'*Macbeth* in a provincial town' was commissioned by the Bear Gardens Museum and Arts Centre and appeared in *Poems for Shakespeare, 8*.
'An island story' appeared in *Alderney: A book of poems*.
Acknowledgements are also due to Faber and Faber Ltd for permission to quote from *The Inheritors* by William Golding.